THE SCOTSMAN

Collins

SCOTTISH

PLACE NAMES

D0995402

Collins

HarperCollins Publishers
Westerhill Road
Bishopbriggs
Glasgow
G64 2QT

www.collinslanguage.com

First Edition 2009

This edition created exclusively
for The Scotsman

ISBN 978-0-00-785215-4

Text © John Abernethy 2009

Illustrations © Alex Collier 2009

The moral rights of the author
have been asserted

The moral rights of the illustrator
have been asserted

Collins® is a registered
trademark of HarperCollins
Publishers Limited

A catalogue record for this book
is available from the British
Library.

Designed and typeset by
Thomas Callan

Printed and bound in Great
Britain by Clays Ltd, St Ives plc

Editorial Staff
Ian Brookes
Helen Hucker
Robert Groves

For the Publishers
Lucy Cooper
Elaine Higgleton

Introduction

The history of Scottish place names is as fascinating as the history of Scotland itself, and indeed the two subjects are inextricably intertwined. Scotland has been settled by Celts, Britons, Picts, Angles, Irish, Vikings, Normans, and English (amongst others) and the place names of Scotland mirror that diverse heritage. Glasgow and Edinburgh come from completely different linguistic traditions – Glasgow from old Celtic Brythonic (the southern branch of Celtic languages) and Edinburgh from Old English. Even the name 'Scotland' itself is formed by tacking the English word *land* on to the Latin *Scotti*, a word with the rather uncomplimentary meaning of 'pirates', which was given to the Irish people who settled in the west of Scotland around AD500 and would later give their name to an entire nation.

There is a smorgasbord of Scandinavian names in places ranging from Dumfries and Galloway in the south to the Hebrides in the west and right up to Orkney and Shetland in the far north. This Scandinavian influence is a reminder of the rule of the Norsemen from the 10th century right through to 1469 when the King of Denmark donated Orkney and Shetland to Scotland as a rather unusual wedding dowry for his daughter.

Then, of course, there is the Gaelic tradition. Gaelic was the national language of all of Scotland north of the Forth and Clyde until the 11th century, and it remained the national language of half of Scotland until the depopulation that began to take place in the Highlands and Islands from the 18th century onwards.

And finally we have the English tradition found in Lothian and the Borders. These areas were never Gaelic speaking and were only absorbed into the Scottish nation in 1034, bringing with them a language that would eventually take over the rest of the country. English became the language of the Scottish court in the reign of Malcolm III and Queen Margaret in the 11th century. The united Scottish nation began to use the English name of 'Scotland' rather than the Gaelic name of 'Alba' and the people of the Lowlands of Scotland began to speak their own version of English – Scots.

Within this linguistic melting pot the population of Scotland grew. New villages and towns were built and were given names that derived from Gaelic or Norse or Scots or sometimes a combination of different languages.

In *Scottish Place Names* we take you on a tour of Scotland from the Scandinavian-influenced Northern Isles and the Gaelic-speaking Western Isles, through the stunning Highlands to the historic burghs and industrial towns of the Lowlands. It is a fascinating journey of many languages and cultures, of a country of incomers and invaders, a country of battle, a country of religion, and a country of quite a few steep hills.

This edition is an abridged edition of *Collins Scottish Place Names*, which has been created exclusively for The Scotsman.

Aberdeen

Aberdeen was one of the first of Scotland's royal burghs in the 12th century, and today is the busiest and wealthiest port in Britain. Aberdeen University was established in 1495 and is one of two universities in Aberdeen (the other being The Robert Gordon University).

The name 'Aberdeen' may be a combination of the old Brythonic word *aber* meaning 'where waters meet' or 'the mouth of the river' and *deen* which refers to the River Dee, or else it may come from the old world *Aberdon* ('where the River Don meets the sea') or from *Aberdoen* ('where the Rivers Dee and Don meet each other'). Or perhaps it is from some combination of the three.

Before the advent of oil, Aberdeen was famous for being Scotland's main fishing port. Trawling for white fish began there in 1882. The popular song 'The Northern Lights of Old Aberdeen' refers to the atmospheric phenomenon known as the Aurora Borealis rather than to Aberdeen's vibrant nightlife.

Famous Aberdonians include missionary Mary Slessor, footballer Denis Law, ex-Goodie and *I'm Sorry I Haven't a Clue* stalwart Graeme Garden, and singer Annie Lennox of The Eurythmics, who sang 'Here Comes the Rain Again' (presumably thinking about her home city). The 4th Earl of Aberdeen, George Hamilton-Gordon was British Prime Minister from 1852 to 1855 but resigned after the mismanagement of the Crimean War.

There is another Aberdeen in Washington State, USA, that was the birthplace of Kurt Cobain of Nirvana. Aberdeen is also the name of a famous harbour on the south of Hong Kong Island.

Aberdeen Angus cattle are black beef cattle without horns that were originally bred in Aberdeenshire and Angus.

Aberfeldy

'The Birks of Aberfeldy' is the name of a poem by Robert Burns, and famous people born in Aberfeldy include actor Alan Cumming. The name 'Aberfeldy' derives from the Brythonic *aber* meaning 'where waters meet' and the nearby stream called Pheallaig Burn.

Aboyne

The name 'Aboyne' possibly derives from the Gaelic words *ath* meaning 'ford' and *boinne* meaning 'rippling water'.

Airdrie

Town in North Lanarkshire that grew in the 19th century through the coal and iron industries. The name comes from the Gaelic *airde ruighe* meaning 'high hill slope'.

Alexandria

Largest town in the Vale of Leven in West Dunbartonshire. Alexandria lies on the River Leven and was a former industrial town. Alexandria is not named after the historic city of Alexandria in Egypt, but was named after the then local Member of Parliament, Alexander Smollett, possibly proving that politicians were more highly thought of in the 18th century than they are today.

Alloa

Administrative centre of Clackmannanshire on the north bank

of the River Forth. Alloa used to be a major Scottish brewing town and its name comes from the Gaelic *ailmagh* meaning 'rocky plain'.

Annan

Town and river in south west Scotland. The origin of the name is unknown, although it has been suggested that it simply derives from an old Brythonic name for 'water'. Famous people born in Annan include *Ugly Betty* star Ashley Jensen, but former UN Secretary-General Kofi Annan has no known connection with the town.

The area around Annan is known as Annandale and was where a certain Bruce family were given land and the title of Lord of Annandale in the 13th century before becoming the royal family of Scotland.

Anstruther

Famous people born in Anstruther include Thomas Chalmers, the first Moderator of the Free Church of Scotland (or 'Wee Frees') and Radio 1 DJ Edith Bowman. The name 'Anstruther' derives from the Gaelic *an sruthair* meaning 'the little stream', although locally the town is known as 'Ainster'.

Arbroath

Arbroath is famous for the Declaration of Arbroath, the most important document in Scotland's history, which stated the right of the people of Scotland to independence. The declaration was drafted in support of King Robert the Bruce at Arbroath Abbey on 6th April 1320, with its most famous line being (translated from the original Latin) 'For, as long as but a hundred of us remain alive, never will we on any conditions be brought under English rule.'

On Christmas Day 1950, the Stone of Destiny (traditionally used at the coronation of Scottish monarchs) was audaciously removed from Westminster Abbey. Its captors eventually deposited the stone at Arbroath Abbey (after a spot of repair work to repair the damage incurred during the incident) to mark the importance of this place in Scottish history.

To those with a taste for culinary rather than historical matters, however, Arbroath is famous for the 'Arbroath Smokie', a salted and hot smoked haddock.

Arbroath was a Pictish town with name of Aberbrothock, derived from the Brythonic word *aber* meaning 'mouth of' and *Brothock* the name of local burn that ran into the sea. In Gaelic, *Brothock* becomes *Brothach*, which also means 'turbulent', and the name 'Arbroath' derives from the Gaelic form.

Ardrossan

Ardrossan is best known as the place where you catch the ferry to sail to the island of Arran. The name 'Ardrossan' perhaps derives from the Gaelic *airde ros an* with *airde* meaning 'height', *ros* meaning 'headland' or 'promontory', and *an* meaning 'little'.

Arran

A popular tourist destination, with aspects resembling both the Lowlands and the Highlands, Arran has been described as being 'Scotland in Miniature'.

Arran takes its name from the Gaelic *Arainn* or Brythonic *Aran*, both of which mean 'place of high peaks'. Arran has also in recent years joined the likes of Lewis, Harris, Skye, and Iona as one of the Scottish place names that is also a popular first name.

Aviemore

Aviemore was developed in the 1960s to become Scotland's first centre for winter sports, although continued lack of snow has understandably proved a problem for a place attempting to establish itself as a premier skiing resort. The name derives from the Gaelic *agaidh* meaning 'pass' and *mor* meaning 'big' and is therefore 'big pass'.

Ayr

Ayr has been a royal burgh since the 13th century and is well known for tourism, horse-racing (Ayr racecourse being the home of the Scottish Grand National), and through its connections to Robert Burns, who was born only two miles away in the village of Alloway. Burns once wrote of the people of Ayr in the epic poem *Tam o' Shanter*:

> *Auld Ayr wham ne'ar a toun surpasses*
> *For honest men and bonnie lassies*

… and Burns certainly knew quite a few of the latter.

Other famous people from Ayr include engineer John Loudon McAdam, who revolutionized road building with what would be named 'tarmacadam' in his honour.

Ayr took its name from the River Ayr at whose mouth the town was built. The origin of the name is unknown, although it is almost certainly of Brythonic origin.

Ayrshire is the greater region around Ayr and is divided into three local-government authorities: East Ayrshire, North

Ayrshire and South Ayrshire. Much of Ayrshire is farming country and the Ayrshire is a breed of dairy cattle.

Ballater

Ballater was originally a spa town before becoming associated with the royal family from the 19th century onwards. As the nearest town to Balmoral it has become one of the most popular tourist destinations in Royal Deeside. The origins of the word 'Ballater' are not certain, although the name could derive from the Gaelic word *bealach* meaning 'mountain pass'. Famous people born in Ballater include pioneering town planner Patrick Geddes.

Banchory

Banchory has become a commuter town serving Aberdeen and is often called 'The Gateway to Royal Deeside'. The name 'Banchory' is of disputed origin: it is suggested that it either derives from the Gaelic *beannach* meaning 'forked' (in reference to its location on the River Dee) or else from the Gaelic *beannchar* meaning 'blessed place' as a reference to the 6th-centrury Saint Ternan who is said to have brought Christianity to the region. Indeed, until relatively recent times the town was called Banchory Ternan.

Banff

The town of Banff dates back at least to the 12th century, and its name either derives from the Gaelic *banbh* or *banbha* and could mean either 'land left fallow', 'a stream', or 'a pig'. The name of Banff and Buchan has recently become famous for being the long-standing parliamentary constituency of

Scotland's First Minister, Alex Salmond, a man who has no doubt enjoyed an occasional bacon roll in his time.

Banff is also the name of a resort town in Alberta's Rocky Mountains, and the Canadian Banff now has a larger population than the Scottish town after which it was named.

Barrhead

Barrhead became known for the manufacture of textiles and toilets. The name is thought to be Scots in origin, with *barr* being Scots for 'ploughed furrows' (rather than coming from the Gaelic word *barr* meaning 'hilltop'), and the original settlement of Barrhead was built at the head of the ploughed fields. Famous people born in Barrhead include Scottish footballer and manager Alex McLeish.

Bathgate

The name 'Bathgate' does not derive from either a bath or a gate, but from the Brythonic *baedd coed* meaning 'boar wood', harking back to a time when boars lived locally. Famous people born in Bathgate include pioneering doctor James Simpson, *Doctor Who* actor David Tennant, and motor racing driver Dario Franchitti.

Bearsden

Bearsden is built on the site of the Antonine Wall with several sections of the Wall still visible t oday. Bearsden was previously called first New Kilpatrick and then New Kirk, before the building of today's town began in the 19th century. The current name was taken from the local railway station, which was in turn named after a nearby house, although it is unclear what the original significance of the name might have been. There is certainly little evidence of bears in this prosperous area.

Beauly

The name 'Beauly' is French in origin, coming from the 13th-century Beauly Priory that was founded by French monks who gave it the name of *beau lieu* ('beautiful place').

The Beauly Firth is the inlet of the sea that goes from Beauly in the west to Inverness in the east where it enters the Moray Firth.

Bellshill

The town was first called Bellshill in the 19th century and was built on a hill on the site of a village formerly known as Bellmill, after a Mr Bell who owned a stone quarry there. Famous people born in Bellshill include Labour politician Robin Cook, singer Sheena Easton, and footballer Ally McCoist.

Biggar

The name might derive from the Norse *bygg* meaning 'barley' and *gardr* meaning 'field'. The town of Biggar gave its name to the surname Biggar and in turn became the subject of the tongue-twisting question 'Mrs Biggar had a baby boy. Who was bigger – Mrs Biggar or her baby?' The answer, of course, being the baby, as he was 'a little Biggar'.

Bishopbriggs

Bishopbriggs was mostly built from the 19th century onwards and is a commuter town serving Glasgow. The name derives from land given to the Bishop of Glasgow, although there is argument about whether the second element refers to *briggs* (the Scots word for 'bridges') or *riggs* (the Scots word for 'fields'). Bishopbriggs is also home to the publishers HarperCollins, noted for their excellent dictionaries and books about Scotland.

Blair Atholl

Picturesque town in Perthshire, with the seat of the Duke of Atholl, Blair Castle, nearby. The name means 'the field of the new Ireland' with *blair* in Gaelic meaning 'field' or 'plain' and *Atholl* historically meaning 'New Ireland'.

Blairgowrie

Town in Perth and Kinross, known for growing raspberries. The name 'Blairgowrie' means 'the plain of Gowrie', but the origin of the place name 'Gowrie' is unclear.

Blantyre

Blantyre is famous for being the birthplace of African explorer and missionary David Livingstone. There is a much larger Blantyre in Malawi, the largest city in that country, with a population of over 700,000, which was named in honour of Livingstone's birthplace in 1891.

The name 'Blantyre' is of Brythonic origin and is believed to derive from *blaen tir* meaning 'edge of the land', in recognition to the area's proximity to the River Clyde.

Bonnybridge

Bonnybridge is famous for having more UFO sightings than anywhere else in Scotland. The name does not, sadly, derive from the town being 'bonny' in the Scots sense, or even an extra-terrestrial sense, but from the Gaelic *buan* meaning 'swift', a word that refers to the Bonny Water that was crossed by a bridge here.

Bo'ness

Former major port and town in West Lothian on the Firth of Forth, near the eastern end of the Antonine Wall. 'Bo'ness' is a contraction of the town's former and considerably less catchy name of Borrowstounness. That name derived from an Old English first name *Beornweard,* the Old English *tun* meaning 'farm', and the Old English *naes* meaning 'headland'.

Braemar

Braemar is famous for the Braemar Gathering, the Highland Games held since 1832 and traditionally attended by the Royal Family. It was at Braemar that the Jacobite standard was raised for the unsuccessful 1715 uprising. The name derives from the Gaelic *braigh* meaning 'uplands', although the meaning of *Mar,* which is also the root of the Scottish surname Marr, is unknown.

Brechin

Brechin is famous for its 14th-century cathedral that incorporates an even earlier round tower. Famous people born in Brechin include radar pioneer Robert Watson-Watt.

The origin of 'Brechin' is unclear, but it is possibly a Pictish or Brythonic name derived from a person called Brychan or Brachan.

Buckie

The name 'Buckie' is thought to derive from either *bocaidh*, the Gaelic word for 'whelk', or *buckie*, the Scots word for 'whelk'. The Fife fishing town of Buckhaven could have the same gastropodous origins.

Callander

The name 'Callander' is of uncertain origin, but possibly shares the same derivation as Calder (explained in the previous entry). Callander became better known in the 1960s as the location for the fictional town of Tannochbrae, the setting for *Doctor Finlay's Casebook*.

Cambuslang

The name 'Cambuslang' derives from the Gaelic *camus* meaning 'bay' and *luinge* meaning 'ship'. The name refers to the fact that boats or ships could sail up the River Clyde to the original settlement.

Carluke

The first part of the name derives from the Brythonic *caer* meaning 'fort', but it is unclear what *luke* means. It seems unlikely, however, that is has any connection with the biblical Saint Luke.

Carnoustie

Carnoustie has hosted the Open Golf Championship seven times and is sometimes nicknamed 'Carnasty' because of the perceived difficulty of the course.

The meaning of 'Carnoustie' is disputed: it may derive from the Gaelic *carn fheusta* meaning 'cairn of the feast' or else from *carn ghiutasiach* meaning 'cairn of the pine trees'.

Clackmannan

The name comes from the Gaelic *clach manna* meaning 'stone of Manau', with the meaning of 'Manau' being unknown, although it is probably a person's name.

Clydebank

The town was almost completely destroyed by the Luftwaffe in 1941 during the Second World War. Clydebank is also where the group Wet Wet Wet hail from, and is apparently a romantic place as 'Love Is All Around'.

Coatbridge

Coatbridge grew in the 19th century through the coal, iron, and steel industries. The name means literally 'bridge built next to cottages', as *cotts* is an old English word for 'cottages'.

Coldstream

Coldstream has long been a border crossing point to England and is best known for the Coldstream Guards, a regiment of the Household Division of the British Army, which has been in active service since its founding in 1650. The regiment was founded in Coldstream as part of the English Parliament's 'New Model Army' at the time of the English Civil War, and in 1658 moved from Coldstream to London to help bring about the restoration of the Stuart monarchy. As part of their duties the Coldstream Guards guard the royal properties in London, such as Windsor Castle and Buckingham Palace.

The name 'Coldstream' is, as you might imagine, a reference to the temperature of the River Tweed.

Cowdenbeath

The name possibly derives from a person called Cowden, combined with the Gaelic word *beith* meaning 'birches'.

Crianlarich

Crianlarich is best known for being a popular stopping-off point for tourists en route to the North and West Highlands. The name 'Crianlarich' derives from the Gaelic *crion* meaning 'little' and *lairig* meaning 'pass'.

Crieff

The name 'Crieff' means 'place among the trees', deriving from the Gaelic *craoibh* meaning 'trees'. Famous people born in Crieff include film star Ewan McGregor and his actor uncle Denis Lawson who starred in the film *Local Hero*.

Culross

The town was formerly an important trading port and is the possible birthplace of the patron saint of Glasgow, Saint Kentigern, who was better known as Saint Mungo. The name 'Culross' possibly means 'holly wood', deriving from the Gaelic *culeann* meaning 'holly' and the Brythonic *ros* meaning 'wood' (although the second part of the name could also perhaps be derived from the Gaelic *ros* meaning 'point').

Cumbernauld

Cumbernauld was previously a village with the name coming from the Gaelic *commain nan allt* meaning 'where the streams meet' as it is situated between streams that flow into both the Clyde and the Forth. Cumbernauld is known for its self-promotional catchphrase 'What's it called? Cumbernauld!' and was also the setting for the 1981 film *Gregory's Girl*, which depicted a teenage boy's infatuation with a girl who played in his school football team. The football team Clyde plays at Cumbernauld, but Dee Hepburn will not be found among its players.

Cumnock

Cumnock was formerly an important mining area. The name possibly derives from the Gaelic *cam cnoc* meaning 'crooked hill'.

Cupar

The name 'Cupar' is of uncertain origin, although it has been suggested that it derives from the Gaelic *comhpairt* meaning 'common grazing land'.

The smaller town of Coupar Angus is so named to differentiate it from the Fife town of Cupar, although confusingly Coupar Angus is not actually in Angus, but in Perth and Kinross.

Dalkeith

Dalkeith takes its name from the Brythonic *dol coed* meaning 'field by the wood'. Dalkeith Palace was the residence of the Dukes of Buccleuch. Famous people born in Dalkeith include 18th-century politician Henry Dundas, known as the 'uncrowned king of Scotland', and Fish, lead singer of the rock group Marillion.

Dingwall

Dingwall derives its name from the Norse *thing vollr*, with *thing* meaning 'assembly' or 'parliament' and *vollr* meaning 'field'. A similar Norse name *Tynwald* is the name of the parliament of the Isle of Man. Famous people born in Dingwall include the Scottish king Macbeth.

Dornoch

Dornoch Firth is the name of a sea inlet that separates Sutherland from Ross and Cromarty with Dornoch on its north shore.

The name 'Dornoch' derives from the Gaelic *dornach* meaning 'pebbles' – although today the beaches are mostly sandy.

Dufftown

The town was named after James Duff, the fifth Earl of Fife, who founded it in 1817. Duff was a member of the Clan MacDuff, who long held the title of Thane of Fife (and feature as such in William Shakespeare's *Macbeth*). The surname 'Duff' derives from the Gaelic *duibh* meaning 'black'.

Dumbarton

Dumbarton was the capital of Strathclyde, an ancient kingdom of the Britons, from the 5th century until it was added to Scotland in the 11th century. The kingdom was ruled from a royal castle and fortress that sat on top of Dumbarton Rock. Dumbarton would later become a shipbuilding town and its famous sons include Jackie Stewart, the former world motor-racing champion, and David Byrne, the lead singer of Talking Heads.

Dumbarton should technically be called 'Dunbarton' as the name comes from the Gaelic *dun breatainn* meaning 'fort of the Britons'. The Britons themselves called their capital 'Alcluith' meaning 'rock of the Clyde'.

The region around Dumbarton is actually called 'Dunbartonshire' rather than 'Dumbartonshire' and is divided into two local-government regions: East Dunbartonshire and West Dunbartonshire.

Dumfries

Dumfries Kirk was where Robert the Bruce killed John Comyn, his main rival to the vacant Scottish throne, in 1306 and was where Robert Burns was buried after his death in 1796. Dumfries is also the place where the inventor Kirkpatrick Macmillan is believed to have ridden the first ever bicycle in 1839. The name is believed to mean 'ridge of the thicket' (if one takes *dum* as deriving from the Gaelic *drum* meaning 'ridge'). However, if *dum* derives from the Gaelic *dun*, then 'Dumfries' is more likely to mean 'fortified woodland'.

Dumfries has the nickname of 'The Queen of the South', which is also the name of the local football club. People from Dumfries are called 'Doonhamers', from a Scots expression for 'down south', since its location at the southern end of Scotland means that there is nowhere further down for you to go.

Famous people born in Dumfries include the broadcaster Kirsty Wark.

Dunbar

Dunbar derives its name from the Brythonic *din* meaning 'fort' and *barr* meaning 'height' or 'summit'. Dunbar was the location of a battle in 1650 when Oliver Cromwell's English army, despite being heavily outnumbered, defeated the Scots and proceeded to occupy the entire country.

Famous people born in Dunbar include pioneering conservationist John Muir. Dunbar is said to have more sunshine than any other place in Scotland and has therefore gained the nickname of 'Sunny Dunny'.

Dunblane

The name 'Dunblane' means 'fort of Saint Blane' after the 6th-century Irish Saint Blane. Famous people born in the town include tennis players Andy and Jamie Murray.

Dundee

Dundee possibly took its name from the Gaelic word *dun* meaning 'hill' or 'hill-fort' and the Gaelic word *deagh* meaning 'fire', perhaps in recognition of the beacons that were lit on Dundee's highest point, the Dundee Law. Other possible translations of the city's name include 'dark hill'.

Dunfermline

Dunfermline is one of Scotland's earliest royal burghs and a royal residence from the 11th to the 17th century. Famous people born in Dunfermline include Charles I, king of England and Scotland from 1625 until his execution in 1649, Andrew Carnegie, who made his name in America as a steel magnate and philanthropist, and who gave his name to the Carnegie

Hall, and singer and actress Barbara Dickson, who had an international hit with 'I Know Him So Well'.

Dunfermline takes its name from the Gaelic *dun fearam linn* that means 'the fort in the bend of the stream'.

Dunkeld

The relics of Saint Columba were brought to Dunkeld in the 9th century, and Dunkeld Cathedral was built over the site of his burial in the 12th century. Dunkeld was an important royal and religious centre in medieval Scotland and gave its name to the royal House of Dunkeld that held the monarchy from 1034, when Duncan I became the first king of a unified Scotland, to the death of Margaret the Maid in 1290.

The name 'Dunkeld' derives from the Gaelic and Pictish *dun* meaning 'fort' and the Gaelic *chailleainn* meaning 'of the Caledonions'.

Dunoon

The town of Dunoon is next to Holy Loch, which was a controversial, if locally lucrative, American navy base from 1961 to 1992. The name 'Dunoon' derives from the Gaelic *dun* meaning 'fort' and *obhainn* meaning 'river'.

Duns

The proud motto of the town is 'Duns dings a'' meaning 'Duns beats all', and people from Duns are called 'Dingers'. The name 'Duns' derives from the Gaelic *dun* meaning 'fort on the hill', and the original settlement of Duns was built on top of the hill called Duns Law.

Famous people born in Duns include acclaimed 13th-century theologian and philosopher John Duns Scotus. Over time, however, his views fell out of fashion and his supporters, who were called Dunses after the town of his birthplace, began to be criticized. Hence the origin of the term 'dunce' being used as a derogatory term for those considered incapable of becoming good scholars. It is not surprising, therefore, that the educated and wise people of Duns were so keen on having an alternative nickname – even if it happened to be 'Dingers'.

East Kilbride

East Kilbride was a village until 1947 when development began on turning it into Scotland's largest town – only the cities of Glasgow, Edinburgh, Aberdeen, and Dundee having a larger population.

The name 'Kilbride' comes from the Gaelic meaning 'the church of Saint Bride'. Saint Bride or Saint Bridget was a 5th-century Irish nun known for her holiness and founding several convents in Ireland. Bride was also the name of a Celtic goddess of fire, and the preservation of the pagan name reflects the fact that the early Celtic church retained many of the pre-Christian religious traditions.

East Kilbride was so named to differentiate it from the village of West Kilbride that is found in Ayrshire. Famous people born in East Kilbride include television presenters Lorraine Kelly and Kirsty Young, who have both presented *Have I Got News for You*.

Edinburgh

Edinburgh used to be a Northumbrian town and was ruled by the Angles until captured by the Scots in 1018. Edinburgh's Gaelic name is *Dun Eideann*. *Dun* means 'hill fort', but what *Edin* meant in its original Northumbrian is unclear, although it might mean 'rock face' or be the personal name of a king or ruler. It has been suggested that *Edin* might refer to a Northumbrian king called Edwin, but the name of *Dun Edin* predates the 7th century, when Edwin lived, so this is thought unlikely. *Burgh* is an English word meaning 'stronghold' or 'town' and the English word *Edinburgh* was used rather the Gaelic *Dun Eideann*. The Gaelic name was, however, taken up as the name of the city of Dunedin in New Zealand's South Island, and that city also shares many of Edinburgh's famous street names.

Edinburgh gained the nickname 'Auld Reekie' after the amount of smoke that would fill the sky on the occasions when the residents lit their coal fires and was also called 'The Athens of the North' in recognition of its dramatic historic landscape and the failed attempts to replicate a Greek style Acropolis on Calton Hill.

Famous people born in Edinburgh included James VI of Scotland, who became James I of England in 1603, renowned philosopher David Hume, renowned scientist James Clerk Maxwell, inventor of the telephone Alexander Graham Bell, leader of Dublin's 1916 Easter Rising James Connolly, birth-control pioneer Marie Stopes, film legend Sean Connery (who liked his Edinburgh accent so much that he kept it no matter what nationality of character he was playing), British Prime

Minister Tony Blair, and 19th-century Skye terrier Greyfriars'
Bobby (who may not have been born in Edinburgh, but whose
gravestone and statue are amongst the most visited places in
the city). Edinburgh is also known for being the birthplace
of famous authors Sir Walter Scott, Robert Louis Stevenson,
Muriel Spark, and Irvine Welsh, and is the home of bestselling
writers J.K. Rowling, Ian Rankin, and Alexander McCall Smith.

Eigg

In 1997 the 80 or so residents of Eigg successfully completed
a community buy-out of the island. The name 'Eigg' does not
have any connection with eggs but possibly derives from the
Gaelic *eag* meaning 'notch' or 'rift' in reference to the ridge that
runs down the island from its highest point.

Elgin

A much larger Elgin (with a population of 100,000) is to
be found in the American state of Illinois. The name is also
famously associated with the Elgin Marbles, a collection of
marble sculptures and ancient antiquities from the Acropolis
in Athens that was appropriated by Thomas Bruce, the 7th
Earl of Elgin, in the early 19th century, and which the British
Government has consistently refused to return to Greece.

Elgin probably takes its name from the Gaelic word *elg* meaning
'Ireland', which would make Elgin 'Little Ireland'.

Ellon

The name 'Ellon' derives from the Gaelic *eilean* meaning
'island', referring to the fact that the town was built on a ford of
the River Ythan.

Eriskay

It was at Eriskay that Charles Edward Stewart first landed on Scottish soil in 1745 with thoughts of reclaiming the British crown, and in 1941 the *SS Politician* ran aground there with a cargo of whisky, so inspiring the Compton Mackenzie novel *Whisky Galore*. The name 'Eriskay' is Norse in origin and means 'Erik's island'.

Erskine

The town is best known for the Erskine Bridge, built in 1971, that connects Dunbartonshire on the north bank of the Clyde to Renfrewshire on the south bank. The name 'Erskine' possibly derives from the Gaelic *ard sescenn* and means 'high marsh'.

Falkirk

Two major battles took place at Falkirk: Bonnie Prince Charlie's Jacobites won a rare victory there in 1746, but in 1298 William Wallace's brief tenure as Guardian of Scotland came to an end there when the Scottish forces were defeated by the English forcing Wallace to go in to hiding.

Falkirk is today famous for the Falkirk Wheel, a rotating boatlift that opened in 2002, and for being one of the stops on the train line between Edinburgh and Glasgow. Fortunately, it is not compulsory to get off the train there.

The *kirk* in 'Falkirk' comes from the Scots word for 'church' and *fal* means 'field' or 'fold' so Falkirk is 'the field near the church'. The Gaelic name is *An Eaglais Bhreac*, which means 'the speckled church'.

Forfar

Forfar is famous for giving its name to the Forfar bridie, a meat pastry with optional onions, supposed to have been given its name as it was cooked as a dish to be eaten at wedding meals (which also explains the horseshoe shape of the pastry). The name 'Forfar' itself possibly derives from the Gaelic *faithir faire* meaning 'lookout hill'.

Forres

According to William Shakespeare's *Macbeth*, Forres was the location of King Duncan's castle. The name 'Forres' is believed to be identical with the name *Varris* recorded by the Romans. However, the Gaelic name *Farrais* means 'beneath the bushes', a reference to the town's location at the foot of forested hills.

Fort William

Fort William is a popular tourist destination due to its proximity to Ben Nevis and Glencoe and is the finishing line for walkers completing the West Highland Way. The town was built by Cromwell's troops in the 1650s at the time of the English occupation and was named 'Fort William' after King William III in the 1690s.

The town was then renamed first 'Gordonsburgh' and then 'Duncansburgh' before reverting to its original name after the Jacobite risings – this time in honour of Prince William, the Duke of Cumberland (the same man after whom Fort Augustus had been named). The Gaelic name for Fort William is *An Gearasdan*, which simply means 'The Garrison'.

Fraserburgh

Fraserburgh takes its name from the Fraser family, local landowners who built the town in the 16th century. The town is known locally as 'The Broch', a Scots variation of 'burgh'.

Galashiels

Known locally as simply 'Gala', Galashiels is noted for textile industries and rugby. The name derives from the Gala Water, on which the town is situated, and the Norse word *skalis* meaning 'shieldings' or 'sheds'. The name 'Gala' itself is believed to come from the Brythonic *gal gwy* meaning 'clear stream'.

The motto of Galashiels is 'soor plooms' and is said to refer to an incident in the 14th century when English raiders were defeated in a field of plum trees. The phrase was later applied to a sharp-flavoured sweet.

Giffnock

The name 'Giffnock' derives from the Brythonic *cefn* meaning 'ridge' and *oc* meaning 'little'.

Girvan

Girvan was once a popular holiday destination for Glaswegians in the days before cheap air travel to the Mediterranean. Boats from Girvan run to the nearby island of Ailsa Craig in the Firth of Clyde. There is no agreement on where the name 'Girvan' comes from, although it has been suggested that it may derive from the Brythonic word *gerw* meaning 'rough', although (as you might imagine) residents of Girvan are not especially keen on that translation.

Glasgow

Glasgow was founded in the 6th century when Saint Kentigern (also known as Saint Mungo) established a church in the kingdom of Strathclyde, then inhabited by Britons. The name 'Glasgow' derives from the Brythonic name *Glascau* meaning 'green hollow' or alternatively 'dear green place'. The latter translation comes from the Gaelic name *Glaschu* and was the name of a classic novel by Archie Hind. To this day locals will call their city 'Glesca' or 'Glesga'.

Glasgow became a burgh in 1175. Its cathedral was built in the 13th century and Glasgow University was founded in 1451 (other universities in Glasgow are Strathclyde and Caledonian University). In the 19th century Glasgow became one of the most important industrial cities in the world, at the forefront of the steel and shipbuilding industries, and gave itself the title of 'Second City of the British Empire', hosting the Empire Exhibition of 1938. The popular song 'I Belong to Glasgow' was written by entertainer Will Fyffe.

Glenrothes

Glenrothes was Scotland's second new town when it was founded in 1949. The name 'Glenrothes' derives from the Earls of Rothes, who were local landowners in Fife. The Earls of Rothes were Leslies who also owned land in north-east Scotland and took their name from the Moray town of Rothes, whose name means 'ringed fort' (from the Gaelic word *rath*). The *Glen* part of the name was added to differentiate the Fife Rothes from the Moray Rothes, even though there is no glen as such – although the town is in the Leven valley.

Glenrothes has proved successful in attracting electronic and new-technology industries to the area and is often associated with the phrase 'Silicon Glen', although this term applies more generally to the entire Central Belt of Scotland. Famous people born in Glenrothes include film actor Dougray Scott.

Grangemouth

Grangemouth is home to one of the largest oil refineries in Europe and is also one of the busiest container ports in Britain, with most of Scotland's fuel stocks currently being supplied from there. The town was founded in 1769 to coincide with the construction of the Forth and Clyde Canal and takes its name from the Grange Burn that flows into the Forth, with the name referring to the grange of Newbattle Abbey.

Famous people born in Grangemouth include former *Loose Women* presenter Kaye Adams, although this was in no way a comment on the female population of the town.

Grantown-on-Spey

Grantown-on-Spey was founded on the River Spey by Ludovic Grant in 1765 and was named after the Grant family.

Greenock

Greenock either takes its name from the Gaelic *grianaig* meaning 'sunny bay' or *griancnoc* meaning 'sunny hill'. Famous people born in Greenock include James Watt, whose work on the steam engine ushered in the Industrial Revolution, sea-captain-turned-pirate William Kidd, and actor Richard Wilson.

Laconic comedian Chic Murray was also born in Greenock. Once, when visiting London, Murray was asked by a stranger looking for directions, 'Do you know the Battersea Dogs' Home?' to which he replied, 'I didn't know he was away.'

Haddington

Haddington is a historic town and was one of Scotland's first royal burghs in the 12th century. Its name derives from a personal name *Hada* (of either Old English or Danish origin) and the Old English word *inga* meaning 'people', thus giving a possible meaning of 'town of Hada's people'. Famous people born in Haddington include Scotland's best-known Protestant reformer, John Knox.

Hamilton

Hamilton was previously known as Cadzow but changed its name in honour of James Hamilton, the 1st Lord Hamilton, who died in 1479. The Hamiltons would later become the Douglas-Hamiltons and were given the title of Duke of Hamilton in 1643. Unrelated famous Hamiltons include motor-racing driver Lewis Hamilton.

One of the most famous parliamentary by-elections in Scottish history took place at Hamilton in 1967 when Winnie Ewing won the seat for the Scottish National Party.

There are two larger Hamiltons in the world: Hamilton in Ontario, Canada, has a population of over 600,000, and the city of Hamilton in New Zealand's North Island has a population of over 100,000. Hamilton is also the name of the capital of Bermuda.

The surname Hamilton is not originally Scottish but came from the Anglo-French family of de Hameldon, who also had land in Hambledon in Hampshire. The name 'Hambledon' derives from the Old English *hamel dun* meaning 'crooked hill'.

Harris

Contrary to commonly held belief, Harris is not a separate island, although it is usually referred to as the 'Isle of Harris'.

The Gaelic name for Harris is *Na Hearadh*. However, the name actually comes from the Norse *Haerri* meaning 'higher island' – Harris has more high hills than Lewis to the north – which was anglicized to 'Harris'. The name is quite unrelated to the common English and Welsh surnames Harris and Harrison; those derive from the personal name Henry.

But it was the island that lent its name to the world-famous Harris Tweed, which was hand-woven there from the 19th century onwards. It is something of a curiosity that Harris Tweed takes its name from two Scottish places at completely opposite ends of the country.

Hawick

The name comes from two Old English words, *haga* meaning 'hedge' and *wic* meaning 'settlement', giving us 'hedge settlement'. Famous people from Hawick include rugby commentator Bill McLaren.

Helensburgh

Helensburgh is both a wealthy commuter town serving Glasgow and a popular destination for tourists who wish to see the

Hill House, designed by Charles Rennie Mackintosh, which is located there. Helensburgh was founded in 1776 by Sir James Colquhoun, who built the town along similar lines to Edinburgh's New Town, and named the town in honour of his wife, Lady Helen, Countess of Sutherland.

Famous people born in Helensburgh include John Logie Baird, the inventor of television, and Hollywood film star Deborah Kerr.

Huntly

Huntly was a historic stronghold of the Earls of Huntly and is the site of the ruined 13th-century Huntly Castle. Huntly is associated with the Gordon family and the name 'Huntly' was originally a Borders place name that the Gordons (originally a Borders family) took north with them, first as the name of the castle, and then for the town when it was built in the 18th century. The name derives from the Old English *hunta leah* and means 'hunter's wood'.

Inveraray

Inveraray was built in the 18th century around Inveraray Castle, the family seat of the chief of the Clan Campbell and Duke of Argyll. The 19th-century Inveraray Jail has become an unlikely tourist destination. The name 'Inveraray' derives from the Gaelic *inbhir* meaning 'mouth of the river' and *Aray* the name of the river that enters the loch there.

Invergordon

Invergordon was a base for the Royal Navy until 1956 and is currently the location for oil-rig repairs. The name

'Invergordon' was adopted in honour of the town's founder, Alexander Gordon, in the 18th century, and there is in fact no River Gordon for the town to be at 'the mouth of'.

Inverkeithing

Inverkeithing is best known for being a stopping point for rail services heading north from Edinburgh. The name means 'the mouth of the Keithing Burn', deriving from *inbhir* meaning 'mouth of the river'. The Keithing Burn possibly takes its name from the Brythonic word *coit* meaning 'wood', which would give it the same derivation as the place name and personal name Keith.

Inverness

Inverness became Scotland's fifth city in 2000. *Inver* comes from the Gaelic word *inbhir* meaning 'mouth of the river' and *Ness* from the River Ness (or *Nis* in Gaelic), whose original meaning is unknown. Residents of Inverness are called Invernesians, and famous people born there include Charles Kennedy, deposed leader of the Liberal Democrats. Inverness also features in Shakespeare's *Macbeth* when King Duncan is murdered at Inverness Castle in another act of political treachery.

Inverurie

The name 'Inverurie' means 'mouth of the Ury' with *Inver* deriving from the Gaelic *inbhir*. Inverurie was formerly 'Inverury', but the spelling was changed to help differentiate the town from Inveraray in Argyll.

Iona

Iona has been a spiritual centre from the time when Saint Columba established the first monastery there in 563. It later became a place of pilgrimage and learning, and over 40 of Scotland's earliest kings were buried there, as was Labour leader John Smith in 1994.

The Gaelic name for the island is *Chalium Cille* which translates as 'Saint Columba's Island'. The English name 'Iona' comes from the Norse *ey* meaning 'island' possibly combined with an Irish word *eo* meaning 'the yew tree' (yews having a long association with churches).

Irvine

Irvine had been a port from the 14th century, but was selected in the 1960s to be developed as a new town. Famous people born in Irvine include two politicians of differing persuasions in Jack McConnell and Nicola Sturgeon.

Irvine takes its name from the River Irvine. The name is possibly of Brythonic origin, with *wyn* meaning 'white river', or it may come from the Gaelic *odhar* meaning 'brown river'.

A much larger Irvine is to be found in Orange County, California. That city has a population of over 200,000 people and was named after a family of landowners called Irvine who had emigrated to America from Belfast.

Islay

Islay is today world famous for its whisky distilleries with seven distilleries currently operating on the island, including the famous malts Bowmore, Lagavulin, and Laphroaig. Islay was also famous in Scottish history for being the power-base for centuries for the mighty Clan MacDonald of the Isles. In the 14th and 15th centuries the MacDonalds were also the Lords of the Isles and ruled the whole of the Hebrides from Islay. Famous people born in Islay include Secretary-General of NATO George Robertson.

The name 'Islay' is of Norse origin. The ending comes from *ey* meaning 'island', but the meaning of the first syllable is unclear. It may possibly be from a Norse personal name *Yula*.

Jedburgh

Jedburgh is best known for its ruined 12th-century abbey. The town is built on the Jed Water, from which it gets its name, although locals call the town 'Jeddart' or 'Jethart'. The term 'Jeddart Justice' refers to hanging a man first and then trying him for the crime later (no longer an official policy). Famous people born in Jedburgh include David Brewster, the inventor of the kaleidoscope.

de Groot, who was given a grant in 1496 to run a ferry from the mainland to Orkney.

Johnstone

Johnstone was mainly built in the 18th century, although the place name goes back to medieval times. The name means 'John's settlement'. Famous people born in Johnstone include television chef Gordon Ramsay, although it has to be said that not everybody from Johnstone has quite the same propensity for swearing.

Johnstone is also a popular Scottish surname, a variation of the more common Johnston, which means 'son of John', although some Johnstones will have taken their surname from the town. Famous Johnstones include former Celtic footballer Jimmy 'Jinky' Johnstone.

Jura

Jura is best known for producing Isle of Jura malt whisky and for author George Orwell having lived on the island for three years. The name 'Jura' derives from the Norse *dyr ey* and means 'deer island'.

Keith

The name 'Keith' either derives from the Pictish first name *Cait* or the Brythonic *coit* meaning 'wood'. Keith has become a common surname and boys' first name, with famous Keiths including indestructible Rolling Stones guitarist Keith Richards and the less than indestructible drummer with The Who, the late Keith Moon.

Kelso

The picturesque market town was built around the long-ruined 12th-century Kelso Abbey and a bridge that crossed the River Tweed.

The name 'Kelso' derives from the Old English *calc how* and means 'chalk hill'. The earliest settlement was believed to have been built on a chalky outcrop.

Kilmarnock

The first ever collection of Robert Burns' poetry was published here and was called *The Kilmarnock Edition*. The town is also known for being the home of Johnnie Walker whisky, first sold in Kilmarnock in 1820, and now the most widely distributed blended whisky in the world. The name 'Kilmarnock' comes from *kil*, the Gaelic word for a small Celtic church, and the 5th-century Saint Marnoch. Kilmarnock is often shortened to 'Killie'.

Kilwinning

Kilwinning is the location of a ruined 12th-century abbey and the name has a Christian origin, with *kil* being the Gaelic for 'Celtic church' and *Winning* being derived from either the 6th-century Irish Saint Finian (who taught Saint Columba) or a later and more obscure 8th-century Scottish saint called Winin. Famous people associated with Kilwinning include Bernard de Linton, the man who is believed to have written the most famous document in Scottish history – the 1320 Declaration of Arbroath. De Linton, who was abbot at Kilwinning before he moved to Arbroath, is buried at the abbey.

Kinross

The name 'Kinross' derives from the Gaelic name *Ceann ros*, with *ceann* meaning 'head' and *ros* meaning 'promontory'.

Kirkcaldy

Kirkcaldy is also known as 'The Lang Toun' because of the length of its main street. Kirkcaldy does not take its name from the Scots word *kirk* meaning 'church', but rather from the Brythonic words *caer* (meaning 'fort'), *caled* (meaning 'hard') and *din* (meaning 'hill'), which means the town's name may be translated as 'fort on the hard hill'.

Famous people born in Kirkcaldy include architect Robert Adam, former Liberal leader David Steel, renowned economist Adam Smith, and British Prime Minister Gordon Brown (whose renown as an economist remains to be decided).

Kirkcudbright

The name derives from either the Norse *Kirk Oobrie* or the Gaelic *Chille Cudbert*, both of which mean 'church of Cuthbert' in reference to Saint Cuthbert of Lindisfarne, whose remains were briefly interred in Kirkcudbright. Kirkcudbright is probably most famous for being one of the Scottish place names that visitors find most difficult to say, as none its component parts of 'kirk', 'cud', and 'bright' are heard in the correct pronunciation of 'kir-coo-bree'.

Kirkintilloch

The town lies ten miles north of Glasgow and developed through the construction of the Forth and Clyde canal. It now promotes itself as the 'Canal Capital of Scotland'. Kirkintilloch does not take its name from the Scots word *kirk* meaning 'church', but from the Brythonic *caer* meaning 'fort' and the Gaelic *cinn tulaich* meaning 'at the head of the hill'.

Kirkwall

Kirkwall was the seat of the Norse rulers of the Northern Isles from the 9th century until the 13th century, and it was the Norsemen who built the town's magnificent Saint Magnus Cathedral in memory of the martyred Magnus, Earl of Orkney. The name 'Kirkwall' comes from the Norse *kirkjuvagr* meaning 'church bay', which first became 'Kirkvoe' and then 'Kirkwaa' before being mistakenly translated into English as Kirkwall.

Kirriemuir

Kirriemuir is best known for being the birthplace of *Peter Pan* author J.M. Barrie, who called the town 'Thrums' in many of his novels. Other famous people born in Kirriemuir include Bon Scott, original singer with Australian rock band AC/DC. Film star David Niven claimed to have been born in Kirriemuir, but was in fact born in London.

The name 'Kirriemuir' is derived from the Gaelic *ceathhramh* that means 'quarter', an old Scots term for a measure of land, and *muir*, which is either the Scots for 'moor' or comes from the Gaelic *mor* meaning 'great'. Kirriemuir is often shortened by locals to 'Kirrie'.

Lanark

It was in Lanark that William Wallace began his campaign of resistance by killing the town's English sheriff in 1297. Lanark is also the birthplace of football manager Walter Smith and world rallying champion Colin McRae. Lanark takes its name from the Brythonic word *llanerch* meaning 'forest clearing'. *Lanark* is also the name of a famous novel by Scottish writer Alasdair Gray.

The historic county of Lanarkshire is now divided between the local-government authorities of North Lanarkshire and South Lanarkshire. The area was historically known as a heartland of the Scottish coalmining industry, and remains (just) a heartland of the Scottish Labour Party.

Langholm

The name 'Langholm' derives from the Scots word *lang* meaning 'long' and *holm*, which probably derives from the Norse word *holmr* meaning either 'water meadow' or 'dry land' – although locals call the place 'The Muckle Toon' ('the large town'). Famous people born in Langholm include poet Hugh MacDiarmid, while engineer Thomas Telford was born nearby.

Largs

The Battle of Largs in 1263 is one of the most famous battles in Scottish history. It was fought between Scotland and Norway and marked the end of Norwegian rule over the Western Isles (although nobody is sure who actually won the battle). Famous people born in Largs include golfer Sam Torrance and actress Daniela Nardini, whose family are prominent local ice-cream entrepreneurs. The name 'Largs' derives from the Gaelic *leargaidh* and means 'hill-slope' or 'hillside'.

Lauder

Lauder lies on the Leader Water, from which it takes its name. The valley of the Leader Water is known as Lauderdale.

Lauder is also a Scottish surname and famous Lauders include entertainer Harry Lauder, who became famous around the world for songs such as 'Keep Right On to the End of the Road'.

An even more famous holder of the name is the international cosmetics company Estee Lauder, which sells over 70 perfumes around the world. The company was founded in New York in 1946 by Estee Lauder, who was born Josephine Esther Mentzer before she married one Joseph Lauter and the couple changed their surname to Lauder.

Laurencekirk

Laurencekirk takes its name from a parish called Kirkton of St Laurence, named after the Christian saint. In the late 18th century this parish was amalgamated with another parish called Conveth to form a single village, and Laurencekirk became the name of the new community.

Lerwick

Lerwick is the most northerly town in the United Kingdom and historically was an important fishing port. It is known for hosting the annual Viking midwinter festival of Up-Helly-Aa. The name 'Lerwick' is appropriately Norse and comes from the words *leir vik* meaning 'muddy bay'.

Lesmahagow

The name 'Lesmahagow' is of uncertain origin. It may possibly derive from the Gaelic *lios* meaning 'enclosure', with *mahagow* referring to a 6th-century Welsh saint called Machutus (or Saint Malo) to whom the now-ruined Lesmahagow Priory was dedicated.

Lewis

The Gaelic name for Lewis is *Eileann Leodhas* and so it is often thought that the name comes from the Gaelic *leoghuis* meaning 'marshy'. It is more probable, however, that the name derives from the Old Norse *ljodhus* meaning 'homes of the people'. The anglicized name of the island is unconnected with the

English and Welsh personal name Lewis – that derives from
the French name *Louis*. However, Lewis is currently the most
popular boys' name in Scotland, and these latter-day Lewises
are predominantly named after the Hebridean island. Famous
Scots called Lewis include Lewis Grassic Gibbon, author of
classic novel *Sunset Song*.

The Lewis Chessmen are a collection of 95 chess pieces dating
from the 12th century that were discovered on Lewis in 1831.
They are now on display partly in the British Museum in
London and partly in the National Museum of Scotland in
Edinburgh, which makes it quite difficult to play a game.

Linlithgow

The town is the location of Linlithgow Palace, built in the
15th century, but lacking a roof since 1746. The name derives
from the Brythonic *llyn lleith cau* meaning 'the lake in the wet
hollow'. Residents of Linlithgow are known as 'Black Bitches',
due to the town's crest featuring a black female dog tied to a
tree on an island, a reference to the legend of a faithful dog who
would bring food to her imprisoned master and was tied up by
the authorities to stop her from doing so.

Famous people born in Linlithgow include James V of
Scotland, Mary, Queen of Scots, Scotland's First Minister
Alex Salmond, and Chief Engineer Montgomery Scott of the
Starship Enterprise, who is due to be born there in 2222.

Livingston

Livingston took its name from the old village of Livingston,
which in turn was named either after a 12th-century Flemish

merchant called De Leving or else after an earlier English landowner called Leving.

Lochgilphead

Lochgilphead was built in 1790 to coincide with the building of the road from Inveraray to Campbeltown. The name means what it says, as the town as is at the head of Loch Gilp, an inlet of the larger Loch Fyne.

Lockerbie

The name 'Lockerbie' does not derive from the word *loch*, but from *Locard*, the personal name of a Norse settler in the area. Thus 'Lockerbie' means 'Locard's village', with *bie* deriving from the Norse *by* meaning 'village' or 'settlement'. Locard would also give his name to the popular Scottish surname Lockhart.

Lossiemouth

Lossiemouth was built where the River Lossie flows into the Moray Firth. The river was first recorded in a 2nd-century Roman map with the name of *Loxa*, which is believed to mean 'crooked'. Since 1939 Lossiemouth has been an important base for the Royal Air Force. Famous people born in Lossiemouth include the first British Labour Prime Minister, James Ramsay MacDonald.

Mallaig

Mallaig is the final stop on the West Highland Railway, the final stop on the A830 (better known as 'The Road to the Isles') and the departure point for ferries to Knoydart and many of the smaller Hebridean islands. It is also the main fishing port in the western Highlands. The name 'Mallaig' possibly derives from the Norse *muli vagr* meaning 'headland bay'.

Markinch

The name 'Markinch' derives from the Gaelic words *marc* meaning 'horse' and *innes* meaning 'island' or 'meadow', as it is said that the original settlement was built on an island in a lake that was later drained.

Mauchline

Mauchline is best known for being the setting for many of the poems of Robert Burns, who lived on a farm on the outskirts of the town. William Fisher, an elder of the Mauchline Kirk, was satirized in Burns' poem 'Holy Willie's Prayer', and Jean Armour, the poet's long-suffering wife, was born in the town.

The origin of the name 'Mauchline' is either from the Gaelic *magh* meaning 'field' or 'plain' and *linne* meaning 'pool', or else from *Macha Ruad*, the legendary High Queen of Ireland and goddess.

Melrose

Melrose is famous for the ruined 12th-century Melrose Abbey, where the heart of King Robert the Bruce is buried. The town is overlooked by the Eildon Hills where, according to legend, King Arthur lies sleeping, and nearby Abbotsford was the home of Sir Walter Scott. Melrose is also the place where rugby sevens, the abbreviated form of rugby union, was first played in 1883, and the town hosts the annual Melrose Sevens tournament.

The name 'Melrose' derives from the Brythonic and either means 'bare promontory' (from the words *mail* meaning 'bare' and *ros* meaning 'promontory'), or 'bare meadow' (if the second part comes from *rhos* meaning 'meadow').

Milngavie

Milngavie is the starting point of the West Highland Way. The name 'Milngavie' derives from *muileann* the Gaelic word for 'mill', but it is unclear whether the mill in question belonged to someone called Gavin or someone called David. Today, Milngavie is pronounced 'mill-guy', with the 'v' silent, which was perhaps a compromise, refusing to give either Gavin or David the honour of being the person after whom the town was named.

Moffat

The name 'Moffat' possibly derives from the Gaelic *magh* meaning 'plain' and *fada* meaning 'long'. Moffat is also a Scottish surname, and famous Moffats include *Doctor Who* producer Steven Moffat.

Montrose

Montrose probably takes its name from the former Rossie Island that is now part of Montrose harbour, with 'Rossie' deriving from the Norse word *hrossay* meaning 'horse island'. (Alternatively, the name could derive from the Gaelic *moine* meaning 'peat' or 'moss' and *ros* meaning 'headland' or 'promontory'.) Montrose is famous for James Graham, the 1st Marquis of Montrose, who led the Royalists in Scotland in the Civil Wars of the 1640s.

Motherwell

Motherwell was at the forefront of Scotland's steel industry until the 1980s and their football team is nicknamed 'the Steelmen'. The name comes from a well that was dedicated to the Virgin Mary.

Mull

The origin of the name is unclear, with suggestions ranging from the Gaelic *meal* meaning 'rounded hill', the Gaelic *maol* meaning 'bare summit', or the Norse *muli* meaning 'headland'.

Musselburgh

Musselburgh earned its nickname of 'The Honest Toun' in the 14th century, when the townsfolk refused payment for looking after the ill Earl of Moray, and residents are still known as 'Honest Lads' and 'Honest Lasses'. The town used to be a fishing port, and the name 'Musselburgh' comes from the Old English *musle* meaning 'mussels' and *burgh* meaning 'town'.

Oban

Oban is known as 'The Gateway to the Isles', having ferry connections to many of the Hebridean islands including Mull, Islay, and Barra. The novel and film *Morvern Callar* were set in Oban. The name comes from the Gaelic *An t-Oban* and means 'little bay'.

Orkney

Orkney is famous for its ancient archaeological remains. The site of Skara Brae dates back to 3000BC, making it the oldest evidence of human settlement found in the United Kingdom, and Neolithic Orkney has become a World Heritage Site and popular tourist destination. Orkney was an important Viking earldom or 'jarldom' from the 9th century and was only ceded to Scotland from Norway in 1469. *The Orkneyinga Saga* was a 13th-century history telling the story of the early earls, including Saint Magnus, for whom Saint Magnus Cathedral was built. In both World Wars Orkney provided a major naval British base at Scapa Flow.

The people of Orkney are called Orcadians, and this name harks back to a Roman geographer who referred to the islands as the *Orcades* in the 2nd century AD. The Gaelic name for the islands was *Insi Orc*, which means 'the island of the pigs', but when the Vikings arrived they changed the word *orc* to the Norse word *orkn* meaning 'seal' and called the islands *Orkneyjar* meaning 'seal islands'. That name was later shortened to give its current form. Famous Orcadians include the writer George Mackay Brown.

Paisley

Paisley is the sixth-largest town or city in Scotland, with a population just less than that of East Kilbride. In the 19th century Paisley became known for the distinctive weaving of shawls using a pattern that originated in Iran and India. This pattern became hugely popular and was given the name of the 'Paisley pattern'. The pattern found new popularity in the 1960s and its rock-and-roll image was enhanced when Prince called his recording studio and record label Paisley Park.

Residents from Paisley refer to themselves as 'Buddies', a term that is believed to originate from the word 'bodies' used as a way of referring to people. The name 'Paisley' is thought to be of Brythonic origin, from the word *pasgell* that possibly means 'pasture' – a surprisingly serene meaning for a town that shares a surname with Northern Ireland politician Ian Paisley. Other famous Paisleys include former Liverpool football manager Bob Paisley.

Peebles

The name derives from a Brythonic word *pebyll* meaning 'shielings' or 'sheds'. American singer Ann Peebles had a hit with 'I Can't Stand the Rain', although residents of Peebles are generally much more stoical about the weather.

Penicuik

Until recently Penicuik was known for its paper mills. The name derives from the Brythonic *pen y cog* meaning 'hill of the cuckoo'.

Perth

Perth is one of Scotland's oldest royal burghs and was the capital of Scotland from the 12th century until 1437, when James I was murdered there. Perth is known as 'The Fair City', but in fact is no longer officially classed as a city (although a campaign is now underway to have the title restored). Perth is also known as 'Saint John's Toun' after the 15th-century Saint John's Kirk, and that name is still used today by the Perth football club St Johnstone. Famous people born in Perth include John Buchan, author of *The Thirty Nine Steps*. The name 'Perth' is believed to be a Pictish or Brythonic word meaning 'wood' or 'place of the thicket'.

A much larger Perth is the state capital of Western Australia.

This has a population of over 1,500,000 and is Australia's fourth-largest city.

Peterhead

In the 19th century Peterhead was a major centre of the herring industry, and it remains one of Europe's biggest white-fishing ports. Peterhead is nicknamed 'The Blue Toon' after the blue stockings that the local fishermen used to wear. The town was built in 1587 and took its name from a kirk dedicated to Saint Peter that stood on its headland.

Peterhead fishing skippers were the stars of *Trawlermen*, a television documentary series that had to be subtitled for both English and Scottish viewers so that they could understand the distinctive local Doric accent.

Pitlochry

Now a popular destination for tourists and hill-walkers, Pitlochry developed in the 19th century after the coming of the railway. The name 'Pitlochry' does not derive from the word 'loch' but from the Gaelic *pit cloich aire*. *Pit* derives from the Pictish word *pett* meaning 'place', and the Gaelic *cloich aire* means 'sentinel stone'. This refers to a stone from which it is said that the ancient Picts would observe a nearby Roman fort for possible signs of attack.

Portree

The origin of the name 'Portree' is disputed. It is traditionally said that the name derives from the Gaelic words *port* meaning 'port' or 'harbour' and *right* meaning 'royal' or 'king', making Portree 'the king's port' in recognition of the visit to Skye by James V in 1540. However, another theory is that the *ree* derives from the Gaelic *ruighead* meaning 'slope', therefore making Portree 'the port of the slope'.

Prestwick

Prestwick is famous for being the location for the first twelve Open Golf Championships (from 1860 onwards) and for Prestwick International Airport, first used in 1934 and for many years Scotland's only transatlantic airport. Elvis Presley changed planes here in 1960 when returning from military service in Germany – the only occasion he set foot on British soil. Prestwick Airport is officially called Glasgow Prestwick Airport, even though it is 30 miles away from Glasgow.

The name 'Prestwick' derives from the Old English *preost* meaning 'priest' and *wic* meaning 'farm'.

Raasay

Raasay has long been associated with the Clan MacLeod and famous people born there include poet Sorley MacLeod and crofter Calum MacLeod, about whom the book *Calum's Road* was written. The island's name derives from the Norse *Rarassey* and means 'roe-deer island'.

Renfrew

Renfrew gives its name to the local-government authorities of Renfrewshire and East Renfrewshire. The name is Brythonic, meaning 'point of the current'.

Rosyth

Rosyth is known for the naval base and dockyard that has been based there since 1909. The town was built around the site of the ruined 15th-century Rosyth Castle, and the name derives from the Gaelic word *ros* meaning 'headland' or 'promontory', although it is unclear what the second syllable means.

Rothesay

Rothesay was for many years popular with Glaswegians, who would go 'doon the watter' (down the Firth of Clyde) to spend their summer holidays there. The town has long been associated with the Stewarts (known in Bute as the Stuarts), and from the 14th century the heir to the Scottish throne was given the title of Duke of Rothesay. The ruined Rothesay Castle was also a residence of the Stewart kings. The title of Duke of Rothesay survived both the Union of the Crowns and the fall of the Stewarts, and is still used by the heir to the British crown, with Prince Charles being the current Duke. The name 'Rothesay' derives from the Norse, with *Rotha* being a personal name and *ey* meaning 'island'.

Rum

The island is known for its flora and fauna and is managed by Scottish National Heritage as a National Nature Reserve. The name 'Rum' is of uncertain origin, although it probably means 'wide' or 'spacious' (either from the Gaelic word *rum* meaning 'spacious', or from the Norse *rom ey* meaning 'wide island').

There is sadly no connection between the island of Rum and the alcoholic drink of the same name, and attempts were made to differentiate the two by changing the spelling of the island to 'Rhum', although 'Rum' remains the official name.

Rutherglen

Rutherglen was formerly an important industrial town and historic royal burgh, and actor Robbie Coltrane was born there. The name 'Rutherglen' comes from the Gaelic name *Ruardhgleann* meaning 'red valley' or 'red glen'.

St Andrews

The town became famous from the 9th century onwards as an important Scottish religious centre, having been established in honour of Saint Andrew, a disciple of Jesus and brother of Peter, whose bones were believed to have been taken from Constantinople and buried in Fife. It was also said that Saint Andrew was crucified on a diagonal cross rather than a standard cross, which gave us the Saint Andrew's Cross that became the basis of the Scottish flag. Saint Andrew became the patron saint of Scotland, as well as of Greece and Russia (who presumably also have some of his bones), and his feast day is November 30th.

The 12th century St Andrew's Cathedral, which was at the time the largest building in Scotland, fell into decay in the 17th century, but is still a popular tourist destination. The Royal and Ancient Golf Course was founded in the 19th century and has hosted the Open Golf Championship 28 times, more than any other course. The University of St Andrews remains one of the most prestigious universities in the world, with a certain couple known as William Wales and Katherine Middleton being recent alumni. However St Andrews still does not have a railway station, with the nearest one being at Leuchars, some six miles away.

St Kilda

St Kilda is known as one of Scotland's most famous uninhabited islands, although it is in fact the name for the island group and not the main island. (The main island, which was inhabited for around 2000 years, was called Hirta.) The St Kildans were the most isolated community in Scotland and the final 36 islanders were finally evacuated, at their own request, in 1930. St Kilda is today the location of a defence installation, and is owned by the National Trust of Scotland and has been designated a World Heritage Site.

There has been much discussion of the origin of the name 'St Kilda', as there is no saint called Kilda or anything similar. The name has been used since the 16th century and is believed to have been a misprint by Dutch cartographers for the Norse *skildir* (meaning 'shields', in reference to the shape of the islands) or *Skaldar* (the Norse name for the uninhabited Haskeir Island, which lies between St Kilda and the Outer Hebrides and was wrongly associated with the islands). Another theory is that St Kilda takes its name from the spring called *Childa* on *Hirta*, wrongly thought to have been a holy well and therefore called 'St Kilda'. The archipelago is often known as 'The Islands on the Edge of the World' after the book and film of that name – although the 1936 Michael Powell film was not filmed on St Kilda, but on the remote Shetland island of Foula.

St Kilda is also the name of a popular seaside suburb of Melbourne, home to an Australian Rules Football team. The Melbourne St Kilda is considerably warmer than its North Atlantic counterpart.

Scone

One of the most historic locations in Scotland, Scone was the ancient capital of Alba (the Gaelic kingdom of the Scots and the Picts) from the 9th century to the 11th century, and was the ceremonial coronation site for Scotland's monarchs from Kenneth MacAlpine in the 9th century until James I of Scotland in 1424. In 1651, during the protectorate of Oliver Cromwell, Charles II was crowned King of Scotland at Scone, but had to wait until 1660 before the Restoration of the monarchy was finally complete.

The most precious symbol of the coronation – and of Scotland itself – is the Stone of Destiny (also called the Stone of Scone), a block of sandstone that is said to have been the stone that Jacob slept on in *The Book of Genesis*. The Stone was removed from Scone to Westminster Abbey by Edward I in 1297, and remained there until 1996, when it was returned to Scotland. It is currently on display at Edinburgh Castle (assuming that it is the real Stone and not, as conspiracy theorists have suggested, a copy).

Scone Palace, which still stands today, was built on the site of a former abbey and royal residence by the Earls of Mansfield in the 19th century.

The name 'Scone' derives from the Gaelic *sgonn* and means 'mound'. It is pronounced 'skoon', as opposed to the delicious Scottish cake enjoyed with butter, jam, or cream, which derives from the Gaelic *scon* meaning 'flat' and is pronounced 'skon' or (in refined company) 'skone'.

Selkirk

People from Selkirk are called 'Souters' due to the town's traditional association with shoemaking. Sir Walter Scott was Sheriff in Selkirk, and the *Selkirk Grace* is a verse attributed to Robert Burns and associated with Burns Night. The town's name derives from the Old English *Seles Chirche* meaning 'church in the forest', with the 'church' being changed to the Scots form *kirk*.

Selkirk is also a surname, and famous Selkirks include Scottish castaway Alexander Selkirk, who was the inspiration behind the novel *Robinson Crusoe*.

Shetland

Shetland is the most northerly part of the United Kingdom, 60 miles north of Orkney, and the nearest city is Bergen in Norway. Shetland is famous for its historic archaeology with sites dating back to the Bronze Age. Shetland was ruled by Norway from the 9th century until 1469 when it was ceded to Scotland, but it still commemorates this heritage in the annual Viking festival called Up-Helly-Aa.

Shetland is a major fishing region and from the 1970s onwards became the centre of the North Sea Oil industry, with Britain's largest oil terminal based at Sullom Voe. People from Shetland are called Shetlanders and speak a distinctive dialect partly derived from the Norn language, Shetland's variation of Norse, which was spoken until the 19th century. Famous Shetlanders include former Chancellor of the Exchequer Norman Lamont.

The name 'Shetland' derives from the Norse name *Hjaltland* which means 'hilt land', the hilt referring to the dagger-like shape of the islands. The opening letters 'hj' were replaced with 'sh' and 'Hjaltland' became 'Shetland' (although, with Scots gradually replacing Norn, Shetland gained an alternative English name of 'Zetland', which was the official name of the local council until it reverted to Shetland in 1975).

Shetland is famous for its birdlife and knitwear, and gives its name to several unique animals: the small and popular Shetland pony, the small dog breed called the Shetland sheepdog (which also goes by the name of 'sheltie'), and a small breed of sheep called the Shetland, known for its fine wool. The people of Shetland, however, are mainly of normal height.

Skye

The Gaelic name for Skye is *An t-Eilean Sgitheanach*, which means 'winged island', and the Norse name was *Skuyo*, meaning 'island of mist'.

Staffa

Staffa is famous for its large hexagonal columns or pillars of basalt, the best known being the large sea cave called Fingal's Cave after the Celtic hero Fingal. This became even better known as a result of the *Hebrides Overture* (also known as *Fingal's Cave*) by Felix Mendelssohn, who was inspired by his visit to Staffa in 1829. The name 'Staffa' derives from the Norse *stafr ey* and appropriately means 'island of pillars'.

Stenhousemuir

Stenhousemuir that takes its name from the Old English *stan hus* meaning 'stone house', with *muir*, the Scots word for 'moor' being added later on.

Stirling

Stirling was one of Scotland's first royal burghs and achieved the status of a city in 2002. In medieval times it was Scotland's most important military garrison. William Wallace won a famous battle against the English at Stirling Bridge in 1297, and the 1314 Battle of Bannockburn took place nearby. Stirling boasts a historic castle, dating from the 16th century, and a modern university founded in 1967.

The meaning of the name 'Stirling' is unclear, but it possibly comes from an old Gaelic phrase meaning 'enclosed land by the stream'.

Famous people born in Stirling include former Scotland football captain Billy Bremner. Another sporting legend nominally associated with Stirling is motor-racing driver Stirling Moss, whose name became synonymous with fast driving, so that for decades anybody who was cautioned for speeding would be asked, 'Who do you think you are? Stirling Moss?'

Stonehaven

Stonehaven was formerly a major fishing port and is famous for being the location of the Hogmanay Fireballs Festival and for being the nearest town to Dunnottar Castle. Famous people born in Stonehaven include the first Director-General of the BBC, John Reith. The name 'Stonehaven' is not actually thought to mean 'stone haven'. The town was originally called 'Stonehive', with *hive* possibly deriving from an Old English word *hyth* meaning 'landing place'.

Stornoway

Stornoway is the largest town in the Hebrides and administrative centre of the Na-hEileanan Siar local-government authority. The Gaelic name for Stornoway is *Steornabhagh*, and the town is known for being predominantly Gaelic-speaking and for its strong Presbyterianism and adherence to the Sabbath.

Famous people born in Stornoway include Canadian explorer Alexander MacKenzie. Stornoway was built around a natural harbour and the name derives from the Norse *Stjornavagar* meaning 'steering bay'.

Stranraer

Stranraer is best known for its ferry link to Northern Ireland. The name derives from the Gaelic *sron reamhar* meaning either 'fat nose' or more prosaically 'broad peninsula'.

Strathaven

The name 'Strathaven' means 'wide valley of the Avon' with the Avon being the Avon Water, whose name derives from the Gaelic *abhainn* meaning 'river'. It was near Strathaven that Rudolf Hess bailed out in 1941 in his still-unexplained attempt to visit the Duke of Hamilton in the middle of the Second World War. The name of the town is locally pronounced 'stray-ven', with the letters 'ath' not sounded.

Stromness

Stromness is a ferry port and destination for services from the Scottish mainland. The town takes its name from the

Norse *straumr* meaning 'currents' or 'tides' and *nes* meaning 'headland'. Famous people from Stromness include the writer George Mackay Brown.

Stromness is also the name of the whaling station on the island of South Georgia that was the destination in 1916 for Ernest Shackleton's epic journey to raise help to save his stranded crewmates in Antarctica.

Tain

The name of the town derives from the small river called the Tain Water, whose origin, as with many rivers, is uncertain but probably comes from ancient Brythonic. It may simply mean 'water'.

Thurso

Thurso is the nearest town to the now-decommissioned Dounreay nuclear plant. The name 'Thurso' derives from the Norse *thjors aa* and means 'bull's water'.

Tiree

Tiree is a picturesque and highly fertile island, the latter aspect of its nature being expressed in its name, which comes from the Gaelic *tir eadha* and means 'land of corn'.

Tobermory

Tobermory is famous for its colourful buildings, which were used as the location for the children's television series *Balamory*. The town also appears indirectly in another popular children's television series with Tobermory being the name of one of the characters in *The Wombles*. The name 'Tobermory' derives from the Gaelic name *Tobar Moire* meaning 'Mary's well', referring not to the health of a local resident, but to a well that was dedicated to the Virgin Mary.

Troon

Troon is famous as a holiday resort and for being the location of one Scotland's best known golf courses, which has hosted the Open Championship eight times. The name 'Troon' derives either from the Brythonic *trwyn* meaning 'headland' or from the Gaelic name *An t-Sron* meaning 'the nose', because of its appearance on the map (as compared to Stranraer, further down the coast, whose name in Gaelic means the less complimentary 'the fat nose').

Uddingston

The name 'Uddingston' possibly derives from an Old English or Norse personal name *Oda*, with the name meaning 'the town of Oda's people'. Uddingston is famous for being the home of the Tunnock's confectionery company – world renowned as the maker of magnificent tea cakes and caramel wafers.

Uist

The name 'Uist' derives from the Norse *inni-vist* and means 'a dwelling' or 'an abode'. Famous people from the Uists include national heroine Flora Macdonald, who was born in South Uist.

Ullapool

Ullapool was founded as a herring port in 1788 and was designed by Thomas Telford. It has become a tourist centre and is also a departure point for ferries to Stornoway. Contrary to expectation, the name does not refer to the town's harbour but derives from the Norse *Olaf bolstadr* meaning 'Olaf's farmstead'. This was shortened over time to *Olaf bol* and then anglicized to 'Ullapool'.

Whalsay

Whalsay lies to the east of the Mainland and has recently become the second-largest of the Shetland Islands by population. It is a major fishing community and also boasts the most northerly eighteen-hole golf course in Britain. The name 'Whalsay' is derived from the Norse name *Hvalsey* and means 'whale island' – and if you are lucky you might be able to see whales around the Whalsay coast.

Whithorn

Whithorn is best known for being the location of the first Christian church in Scotland (or at least the first Christian church that we know of), and can lay a plausible claim to being the oldest surviving Scottish town. Saint Ninian is credited with founding a church there around AD400, and this is recorded in Latin as being called *Candida Casa*, which means 'the white house'. This name was then translated into Old English as *hwit erne*, which later became 'Whithorn'.

The nearby fishing village of Isle of Whithorn is actually no longer an island, as a causeway was built to connect it to the mainland in the 1790s.

Wick

Wick was the county town of the former county of Caithness and for a period in the 19th century was the centre of the

Scottish herring industry. The name 'Wick' derives from the Norse word *vik* and means 'bay'.

Wigtown

Wigtown gave its name to the former county of Wigtownshire and has recently been designated as Scotland's National Book Town, with a book festival and numerous bookshops. There is also a place called Wigton in Cumbria, and both names are believed to derive from an English person called Wigca.

Wishaw

Wishaw was formerly at the centre of coal, iron, and steel industries. The meaning of 'Wishaw' is unclear with the *shaw* part being the Scots word for 'wood', but there being no definitive answer as to what the *wi* represents.

Yell

Second-largest island in Shetland by area. Although the wind may blow fiercely there, the name 'Yell' does not have any connections with raised voices, but is derived from the Norse *geldr* meaning 'barren'. Sure enough, two-thirds of the island is covered in peat.

Suggestions for Further Reading

The Scottish Islands: Hamish Haswell-Smith (Canongate)

Tracing Your Scottish Ancestors: Cecil Sinclair (Mercat Press)

Oxford Dictionary of First Names: Patrick Hanks & Flavia Hodges (OUP)

Scottish Place Names: WFH Nicolaisen(Batsford)

Scottish Place Names: David Ross (Birlinn)

Scottish Surnames: George Mackay (Lomond Books)

Bumper Book Of Babies Names: Jacqueline Harrod & Andre Page (Clarion)

Collins Guide to Scots Kith & Kin (Harper Collins)

Scottish Surnames: David Dorward (Mercat Press)

Scotland's Place Names: David Dorward (Mercat Press)

Clans & Tartans: James MacKay (Lomond Books)

Scottish First Names: George MacKay (Lomond Books)

Scottish Christian Names: Leslie Alan Dunkling (Johnson & Bacon)

Illustrated Encyclopedia of Scotland: edited Iseabail MacLeod (Lomond Books)

Collins Encyclopedia of Scotland: John & Julia Keay (Harper Collins)

Surnames of Scotland: George F. Black (Birlinn)

Scottish Names (Harper Collins)

Scottish Words (Harper Collins)